ICONS

JUSTIN TIMBERLAKE

BY BETH GOTTLIEB

Enslow PUBLISHING

Please visit our website, www.enslow.com.
For a free color catalog of all our high-quality books, call toll free 1-800-398-2504 or fax 1-877-980-4454.

Library of Congress Cataloging-in-Publication Data

Names: Gottlieb, Beth, author.
Title: Justin Timberlake / Beth Gottlieb.
Description: Buffalo, NY : Enslow Publishing, 2025. | Series: Icons | Includes index.
Identifiers: LCCN 2024002717 | ISBN 9781978540163 (library binding) | ISBN 9781978540156 (paperback) | ISBN 9781978540170 (ebook)
Subjects: LCSH: Timberlake, Justin, 1981—Juvenile literature. | 'N Sync (Musical group)–Juvenile literature. | Rock musicians–United States–Biography–Juvenile literature.
Classification: LCC ML3930.T58 G67 2025 | DDC 782.42164092 [B]–dc23/eng/20240118
LC record available at https://lccn.loc.gov/2024002717

Portions of this work were originally authored by *Max Maimone* and published as Justin Timberlake. All new material in this edition is authored by Beth Gottlieb.

Published in 2025 by
Enslow Publishing
2544 Clinton Street
Buffalo, NY 14224

Designer: Tanya Dellaccio Keeney
Editor: Kristen Rajczak Nelson

Photo credits: Cover, pp. 13, 15, 19, 21 Featureflash Photo Agency/Shutterstock.com; p. 7 Sipa USA/Alamy.com; p. 9 Tsuni/Alamy.com; p. 11 Album/Alamy.com; p. 17 Abaca Press/Alamy.com; pp. 23, 25 (both) Tinseltown/Shutterstock.com; p. 27 Matt Crossick/Alamy.com; p. 29 AFP/Alamy.com.

Printed in the United States of America

CPSIA compliance information: Batch #CSENS25: For further information contact Enslow Publishing, at 1-800-398-2504.

Contents

Words in the glossary appear in **bold** the first time they are used in the text.

Path to Stardom

From boy-band favorite to **solo** superstar, Justin Timberlake has proven he's an **icon** time and again. He's starred in movies, won awards, and performed on the biggest stages in the world. And it all started when he was just a kid!

ICONIC!

Justin told GQ *in 2013: "It's important to take risks ... To do* ***sketch comedy*** *when you're supposed to be staying in your lane as a singer. To do movies when all people want is your next album. I've made a career out of doing things that I should not be doing."*

Early Life

Justin Randall Timberlake was born on January 31, 1981. He grew up near Memphis, Tennessee. His parents, Lynn and Randall, ended their marriage when he was young. Justin grew up with a stepdad, Paul Harless.

ICONIC!

Justin said he dreamed of making his own music as young as age 10!

On TV

In 1992, Justin appeared on the TV show *Star Search*. He sang a love song. He didn't win the **contest**! One year later, Justin first appeared on *The All-New Mickey Mouse Club* TV show.

ICONIC!

Britney Spears, Christina Aguilera, JC Chasez, and Ryan Gosling appeared on The All-New Mickey Mouse Club *at the same time as Justin.*

Getting the Group Together

In 1995, Justin joined a music group with four other young men. They would come to be called *NSYNC! Their first album came out in the United States in 1998. It featured big hits like "I Want You Back" and "Tearin' Up My Heart."

ICONIC!

*NSYNC's first album came out in Europe first in 1997. They **toured** in Europe and worked on their stage show before the album *NSYNC came out in the United States.

Making It Big

*NSYNC's second album came out in 2000. It was called *No Strings Attached*. It was hugely popular and sold more than 14 million copies! *No Strings Attached* was not only the best-selling album of 2000, but also became one of the fastest-selling albums ever.

ICONIC!

**NSYNC sold the most concert tickets of any music act in 2000 for their No Strings Attached Tour.*

*NSYNC's third album *Celebrity* came out in 2001. Justin showed off his **beat-boxing** skills on the song "Pop." He also co-wrote one of the biggest hits from the album, "Girlfriend." The song's sound and feel showed where Justin wanted to go next in his music.

ICONIC!

NSYNC was **nominated for three Grammy **Awards** for their work on* Celebrity*. They didn't win though.*

Going Solo

In 2002, Justin put out a solo album, *Justified*. At the time, the album didn't mean Justin was leaving *NSYNC. But its R&B and hip-hop sounds were very different from the boy band's music. The album included songs Justin co-wrote, most notably "Cry Me a River."

ICONIC!

Justin won two Grammy Awards for Justified, *including one for "Cry Me a River."*

Justin's second solo album was a huge hit as well. It came out in 2006. He won four Grammys for his work on the album! By then, it was clear *NSYNC had broken up. Justin was a superstar on his own!

ICONIC!

Justin's second album hit No. 1 on the Billboard *charts! It was his first solo No. 1 album.*

ODEON

To the Big Screen

Justin was in his first big movies in 2006 and focused on acting for several years. He was in the award-winning movie *The Social Network* in 2010. He starred in *In Time* in 2011 and appeared in *Inside Llewyn Davis* in 2013, among many others.

ICONIC!

Justin hosted Saturday Night Live *five times between 2003 and 2013. He won four Emmy Awards for his work on the show!*

New Music

Justin's fans finally got new music in 2013. In fact, they got two albums! *The 20/20 Experience* was released, or put out, in two parts that year. Both albums hit No. 1 on the charts!

Jessica Biel

ICONIC!

Justin married Jessica Biel in 2012. They have two sons: Silas and Phineas.

Movie Music

In 2016, Justin voiced Branch in the movie *Trolls*. He also co-wrote the hit song from the movie "Can't Stop the Feeling." It was nominated for an Academy Award! Justin voiced Branch in two more Trolls movies.

ICONIC!

Justin co-wrote "Better Place" for Trolls Band Together. **NSYNC got back together to record it! It came out in 2023.*

Back on Top

Justin released the album *Man of the Woods* in 2018. Again, he hit No. 1 on the charts! The album had a country feel. Justin performed the halftime show at the Super Bowl that year too!

ICONIC!

Justin has worked with many other artists over the years, including Chris Stapleton, Pharrell Williams, the Black Eyed Peas, Nelly Furtado, and Timbaland.

Justin continued to act, starring in several movies. Then, in 2024, fans finally got some new music! *Everything I Thought It Was* came out in March. He then went on a world tour! What will he do next?

ICONIC!

Justin is part-owner of the Memphis Grizzlies basketball team, has put out a clothing line, and been part of other music businesses.

Justin's Music Timeline

1998 *NSYNC *comes out in the United States.*

2000 **NSYNC's* No Strings Attached *becomes one of the fastest-selling albums ever.*

2001 **NSYNC's* Celebrity *comes out.*

2002 *Justin puts out his first solo album,* Justified.

2006 *His second solo album hits No. 1 on the charts!*

2013 The 20/20 Experience *comes out in two parts.*

2016 *"Can't Stop the Feeling," co-written by Justin, is a huge hit.*

2018 *Justin releases* Man of the Woods.

2023 *"Better Place," co-written by Justin and recorded by *NSYNC, comes out.*

2024 Everything I Thought It Was *comes out.*

For More Information

BOOKS

Horning, Nicole. *Justine Timberlake: Musical Megastar*. New York, NY: Lucent Press, 2020.

Timberlake, Justin. *Hindsight & All the Things I Can't See in Front of Me*. New York, NY: Harper Design, an imprint of Harper Collins Publishers, 2018.

WEBSITES

IMDb: Justin Timberlake
https://www.imdb.com/name/nm0005493/
Follow Justin's acting career here.

Justin Timberlake: Official Website
https://justintimberlake.com/
Keep up to date with everything Justin is doing on his website.

Publisher's note to educators and parents: Our editors have carefully reviewed these websites to ensure that they are suitable for students. Many websites change frequently, however, and we cannot guarantee that a site's future contents will continue to meet our high standards of quality and educational value. Be advised that students should be closely supervised whenever they access the internet.

Glossary

award: A prize given for doing something.

beat-box: To use the voice to imitate, or copy, percussion sounds.

contest: A test of skills among people, usually for a prize.

icon: A person who is very successful and admired.

nominate: To suggest someone for an honor.

sketch comedy: A show featuring short, funny skits, which usually aren't part of a larger story.

solo: Alone.

tour: A trip to many places in order to play and sing music for people.

Index